D1394838

PRAGUE CASTLE

PRAGUE CASTLE

OLYMPIA
PRAGUE

Photos © Jiří Kopřiva, 1991
Text © Petr Chotěbor, 1991
Translation © Slavoš Kadečka, 1991

ISBN 80-7033-173-9

The unforgettable panorama of Prague Castle will remain embedded in the memory of every visitor to Prague. Because of its dominant position and its historical significance the Castle has become the symbol of not only the city, but also of the whole state. At the same time it is a unique ensemble of historical buildings and a treasury of rich collections of the most varied works of art.

Its history is long and rich. From its very origin to the present day it has been always the central seat of the administration of the country. This tradition of eleven centuries standing probably has no parallel in Europe. At the beginning it was the seat of Přemyslid princes, later on the residence of Bohemian kings. In the reign of Charles IV and Rudolph II the Castle was even the principal seat of the Emperor of the Holy Roman Empire. For a long subsequent period it was administered by Governors and land administrators. After 1918 it became the residence and place of work of T. G. Masaryk, the first President of the new Czechoslovak Republic, and has been the seat of the head of state ever since.

The Castle has been occupying a strategic place on a rocky mountain ridge above the future city since the end of the 9th century. The few remains preserved from the period of its beginnings could be discovered only by archaeological research. The site of the Castle was then as large as it is today and was fortified with a soil rampart with an interior timber structure. At that time it consisted of small timber houses. The first stone buildings, such as the churches of Virgin Mary, St. George or the rotunda of St. Vitus, were only slow to appear.

The Romanesque period brought about a large scale reconstruction of the Castle. In the first half of the 12th century the former fortified stronghold was rebuilt into a real mediaeval castle with stone palaces, churches and houses. Romanesque fortifications, a stone wall with towers, served the protection of the Castle in the centuries to come. One of the periods of greatest development of the Castle was the reign of Charles IV: the Royal Palace with the All Saints' Chapel was practically newly built and the basilica of St. Vitus, which had replaced the original rotunda, began to give way to a Gothic cathedral.

After the Hussite Wars new construction in the Castle began only in the reign of Vladislav Jagiello. The festive hall, called the Vladislav Hall ever since, ranks among the most beautiful Late Gothic spaces in general. With the ascent of the Hapsburghs (1526) the Castle began changing into a more comfortable Renaissance seat. In its northern outer bailey the Royal Garden was laid out with the beatiful Summer House, the Ballgame Hall and other buildings. In the eastern part of the site the powerful aristocratic families of the Rožmberks and the Pernštejns built their residences. Construction activities of Rudolph II concentrated in the western part of the Castle. This emperor turned the Castle not only into a treasury of his rich collections, but also into a cultural and scientific centre of European fame.

The Baroque style manifested itself in details and interior decorations. Two large scale reconstructions were effected by Maria Theresa in the second half of the 18th century in spite of the fact that at that time Prague was only a temporary seat of the imperial court. First the former Rožmberk Palace was adapted for the Institute of Gentlewomen according to a design by N. Pacassi; subsequently the whole western half of the Castle was rebuilt.

The greatest construction and artistic project of the 19th century was the completion of the St. Vitus' Cathedral the two pseudo-Gothic spires of which enriched the Castle silhouette, which had changed very little in the preceding periods. When the long-neglected Prague Castle became the seat of the President of the Republic in 1918, it was not very well suited for this function. For this reason architect J. Plečnik had been designing and implementing from 1920 a number of modifications, primarily in the gardens, courtyards and representative rooms. Apart from that an extensive reconstruction began in the course of which particulary the modern reconstruction projects of architect Janák were significant. The reconstruction and restoration activities, the endeavour to investigate the history of the Castle, to evaluate its collections of art and to make new buildings accessible to visitors has been proceeding with increasing intensity until the present day.

A FEW INTERESTING DATA ON PRAGUE CASTLE

Castle site:
length 550 m, width max. 170 m
Area, complete with gardens:
267 500 sq. m
The Stag Moat:
width 75—107 m, depth about 30 m
St. Vitus' Cathedral:
length 124 m, west end width 37,5 m, transept width 60 m, vault rise 33 m, west spire height 82 m, main tower height 96, 6 m, height of the golded lion on top of the tower 3 m, weight of the biggest bell, the Sigismund, 18 tonnes
The Vladislav Hall:
length 62 m, width 16 m, vault height 13 m
The Spanish Hall:
length 48 m, width 23 m, height 12 m
The monolith in the Third Courtyard:
height 16,38 m
The Old Castle Steps,
leading to the East Gate,
number exactly one hundred steps
In 1990 the Castle was visited
by 2 338 700 people

FROM HISTORICAL RECORDS CONCERNING PRAGUE CASTLE

1037
When the funereal rites have been properly completed (Jaromír) took his nephew, Břetislav, by the hand and led him to the princely throne, and as it is the custom during the election of the prince, they cast coins over the grilles of the upper hall, ten thousands or even more, among people so they would not oppress the Prince sitting on the throne and rather catch the coins. When the Prince was seated on the throne, there was a big lull. Jaromír, holding his nephew's right hand, said unto the people: "Behold your Prince!"

Cosmas, The Bohemian Chronicle

1060
When Prince Spytihněv (II) arrived in Prague on St. Wenceslas' day, he saw that the St. Vitus' church was not big enough to accommodate all people coming thither for the holy mass — that church had been built once by St. Wenceslas himself to the shape of a Roman church, round, and in it the body of the same St. Wenceslas was laid to rest — and also the second church placed as if in the portico of the first, where on a small area the grave of St. Adalbert lay. He though it would be best to tear them both down and erect one large church for both patron saints. He staked out the new church immediately, laid the foundations, the work grew, the walls rose, but the auspicious beginning were severed next year by his inauspicious death.

Cosmas, The Bohemian Chronicle

1255
When the Prince (later King Přemysl Otakar II) was leaving Prague Castle, an enormous gale started suddenly and the whirlwind threw one rider who was following the Prince from the bridge in front of the Castle; his horse was killed by the fall, but he himslelf escaped unharmed. Also the timber belfry with the bells within the walls (of the Church of Holy Virgin) was torn down in that hour by the strong impact of wind and much other damage was caused in the towns and villages.

Cosmas, The Bohemian Chronicle,
Second Continuation

2nd half of the 13th century
(Přemysl Otakar II) also fortified Prague Castle with particular care by very strong walls, towers and ditches. He placed and covered the walls so that the passage from one tower to another along the whole periphery of the Castle was roofed. He fortified also the Lesser Town of Prague by walls and ditches and adjoined it to the same Castle. In Prague Castle he had ten burgraves, very bold and famous men.

Chronicle of Francis of Prague

1333
We found this Kingdom so devastated that We did not have a single Castle that would not be pledged with all royal estate, so that We had nowhere to dwell but in burghers' houses like other burghers. Prague Castle was so devastated, demolished and broken that since the time of King Otakar II it has fallen to the ground. On that site We had a big and beautiful palace built at great cost as can be perceived today by passers-by.

Charles IV,
Autobiography (Vita Caroli)

1344

Then the new Archbishop of Prague, John, the King of Bohemia, and his two sons, Charles and John, and a great number of prelates and noblemen departed from the Prague church and arrived on the site with the excavated place, prepared for new foundations. Into this excavation four stepped down, viz. the Archbishop, the King and his two sons, and with respect and piety, as appropriate, laid the first stone of the structure of the new church.

Beneš Krabice of Weitmile,
Chronicle of Prague Church

2nd half of the 14th century

At that same time the King (Charles IV) not only augmented the holy services in the Prague Church (St. Vitus' Cathedral), but also the relics of saints. Thus he donated to it the head of St. Ignatius, martyr and bishop . . . and many other diverse relics of apostles, martyrs and confessors, decorated with gold, silver and precious stones, so that no other King of this Kingdom has raised, enriched and honoured the said Prague Church so grandly and magnificantly.

Chronicle of Francis of Prague

1509

That year, at the cost of King Vladislav (Jagiello) a big bell was cast for St. Wenceslas' in Prague Castle, weighing 200 hundredweights, on Wednesday before St. Lawrence (August 8th) in the New Town of Prague . . . And then it was brought to Prague Castle at great cost; because of its great size they broke several cart wheels and subsequently they brought it on a low cart with rollers, and before that arrived to the Castle with it they had to spend five nights in the street. And in the Castle, near the big tower, they had to break a piece of wall between the gates, because they could not pass through the gate for its size.

From ancient Bohemian annals

1541

That famous castle of St. Wenceslas was burnt down to the ground except for the Black Tower which is above the lower gate and in which debtors are usually imprisoned for their debts. The second tower, as is called Daliborka, in which more serious convicts are kept, also remained . . . The excellent chapel of All Saints in front of the Palace, once exquisitely erected at great cost under Emperor Charles and costly decorated with stone carvings and other stonemasons work and beautified with excellent glasses, burnt in and out

ignominiously so that it afforded a horrible and sorry sight to every good man.

Václav Hájek of Libočany,
On evil event . . .

1597

The Emperor's Chamberlains, Hans von Aachen and Bartholomeaus Spranger, both well versed in the art of painting, took me to three castle rooms and showed me the most splendid paintings of old and new times, and most precious that could be seen in any part of Europe at that time. The Emperor (Rudolph II) had them brought thither from all parts of our world at exorbitant cost and expenses . . . Apart from that I saw innumerable vessels of jasper, crystal, alabaster, marble, porphyry and some other rare stones as are found in Bohemia, all moulded most artistically and so exquisitely that it is impossible to state how much they are worth in money.

Jacques Esprinchard,
Report from a Journey

1603

Inside the Castle there is a stable, one of the best equipped in Europe, as it has always some three hundred horses originating from all possible countries, which are most beautiful in the world. Then there is a bestiary with lions, leopards and civet-cats and a raven as white as snow, as well as a ballgame hall in the French manner. The great hall used to be the throne hall of Bohemian Kings. From its windows it is possible to overlook the whole city with the bridge. About nine or ten o'clock numerous gentlemen promenade in that hall and there are also innumerable merchants.

Pierre Bergeron,
Report from a Journey

1612

. . . the above named Abbess has shown and proved before the Commissioners that the previous Abbesses of the same convent had permitted some persons, for a certain sum of money, to build tiny houses on that site which is called Goldsmiths Lane . . . However, some houses were built without permission directly in front of the windows of the convent and the smoke of their chimneys annoys the whole convent. Moreover, food is cooked and beer and wine are sold in several places which gives rise to much disorder and clamour and other improprieties.

Memorial of St. George's Convent

1618

After their departure Slavata and Smečanský first . . . were called the breakers of general peace and good and rebels against the Kingdom of Bohemia in general by Count of Thurn . . . And immediately afterwards a voice was heard from among the Estates that the scoundrels should be put into the Black Tower speedily. Others then called that the traitors should go out of the window . . . And thus, not being permitted any mercy, one after the other . . . with great shouts of "Oh, Oh, Woe!" and with hands clinging to the window frame, which they had to let loose in the end, having been beaten over them, they were thrown, head first, from that same window facing the rising sun, in mantles, with rapiers and other paraphernalia, as they were caught in their office, to the ditch below the palace, deeper than other ditches, separated from it with walls . . . Philip the secretary . . . was thrown out . . . through that same window in their wake. When they all lay down there and were observed to be alive, some mercenary, on the order of Ernfrid of Berbisdorf, fired one or two shots from his gun from the palace window, but missed them. And thus it was a wonder that having been thrown head first from such a height, estimated at 27 ells by some, none of them remained on the spot, but all escaped therefrom.

Pavel Skála of Zhoř,
Bohemian History

1723

The Chief Master of the Hunt, Count Clary-Aldringen, provided for the coronation feast of Charles VI 564 pheasants, 708 partridges, 60 cranes, 152 snipes, 110 quails, 108 hares, 400 fieldfares, the like number of other birds, 70 wild and 60 domestic ducks, 120 turkeys, 350 capons, 70 hens, 800 chickens, 560 pigeons, 50 geese, 30 calves, 46 lambs, 40 rams, 20 fawns and 20 roebucks.

Antonín Novotný,
Prague of the Dark Age

1873

After painstaking work and great endeavour the renovation of the St. Vitus' Cathedral has succeeded so far that on August 30, 1873, when the festival celebrating the 900th jubilee of Prague Bishopric began, the Cathedral was opened again by a festive public service . . .
Not long after this first the second festival, no less important, took place. On October 1, 1873, the foundation stone for the completion of the Cathedral was laid and consecrated, which ceremony was performed personally by his Excellency the Cardinal and Archbishop of Prague. The splendour of the festival was contributed to by all three armed corps of the City of Prague, placed partly in the vicinity of the Cathedral, partly in the courtyards of the Imperial Castle. The foundation stone was placed in the pillar of the transept on the southeast side.

Annual Report
of the Association for the Completion
of the St. Vitus' Cathedral
in Prague Castle

1920

I have a frequent opportunity to see with what piety and love people come to the Castle, eager to learn our millenial stone history. Therefore, soon after my return from abroad, I have taken steps to ensure that by adequate repairs and opening of its various historical components the Castle would become a dignified monument of our history.

T. G. Masaryk

1948

In general Prague Castle and the architect's activities in it differ from the straightforward work of the architect of the present day. Prague Castle has passed through so many presents that they have composed its great complex past. It is not its fault. We observe that for public national life this past, materially useless, has certain values which require preservation. The hundreds of years old layout of Prague Castle has remained valid until the present day. Both for its cultural value and of physical necessity. The plan of Prague Castle has resisted all "improvement" efforts which attacked so powerfully and unintelligently the ancients quarters of Prague in the 19th century and which have cost it so many cultural values. Prague Castle has been preserved and shall be preserved.

Pavel Janák,
The Architect and Prague Castle

The ceremonial entrance to Prague Castle is separated from the Hradčany Square by a grille with sculptures on pillars. The gate is guarded not only by two pairs of Struggling Giants, but also by the soldiers of the Castle Guard. The First Courtyard originated in 1763—1771 during the reconstruction of the Castle in the reign of Maria Theresa. This gigantic reconstruction project converted the mediaeval castle into a dignified mansion with the necessary cour d'honneur, closed by two short wings. In this courtyard official visits of State are received even at present. It is also the site of military parades and at 12 o'clock every day of ceremonial changing of guards.

In the background of the cour d'honneur a valuable architectural monument from the beginning of the 17th century has been preserved — the Matthias Gate, considered the first Early Baroque monument in Prague. Below the cornice of the gateway there are the emblems of the countries under the rule of the Emperor Matthias and situated in the gable is Matthias's imperial coat-of-arms with a festive inscription.

Beyond the gate, on the right, a ceremonial staircase gives access to the first floor, where the representative rooms of the Castle are concentrated. They are decorated with historical furniture, paintings and works of art from the Castle inventory, rare carpets on parquet flooring, gilded chandeliers and stucco ceilings. A remarkable interior can be found in the Hapsburgh Salon with a gallery of paintings representing the members of Maria Theresa family. Some rooms were decorated and furnished in accordance with the designs of J. Plečnik, the first architect of Prague Castle in the Czechoslovak Republic. The number of outstanding interiors includes also the Plečnik's Hall of Columns, the opposite of the Rococo ceremonial staircase leading from the Matthias Gate. The hall affords entrance to two halls from the period of Rudolph II (the Spanish Hall and the Rudolph Gallery). Their present-day appearance dates from the second half of the 19th century, when both interiors were decorated for the coronation of Francis Joseph I which, however, did not take place.

The contemporary appearance of the First Courtyard is also the result of the modifications designed by architect J. Plečnik in 1920—1922 which included also the two flagpoles 25 high.

Two juxtaposed gates bordering the First Castle Courtyard, the cour d'honneur: the grille gate and the ceremonial Matthias Gate leading to the Second Courtyard

The regular
changing of the
Castle Guard is
a favourite sight for
tourists

From the Matthias
Gate the ceremonial
Pacassi's staircase
leads to the
representative
rooms of the Castle
on the first floor
>

The representative rooms are richly decorated with historical furniture and works of art from the Castle collections

The Hapsburgh Salon is a portrait gallery of the members of the family of Empress Maria Theresa

The Brožík's Hall is decorated by the paintings by Václav Brožík, outstanding Czech painter of the 19th century

The Salon of Mirrors is used for official visits of State

The Spanish Hall
was built by
Emperor Rudolph II
at the beginning
of the 17th century.
Its present-day
appearance dates
from 1866—1868

The Rotmayer Hall
connects Plečnik's
Hall of Columns
with the
Spanish Hall
<<

The Salon
of Columns —
a monumental
approach
to the Spanish Hall,
was built to the
design of architect
J. Plečnik
<

The Wedge
Corridor was used
by architect
Nikolaus Pacassi
to level the
irregularities of the
façade of earlier
date. The couple of
columns was
designed by
Otto Rotmayer

The western
entrance gate is
guarded by the
sculptures of
Struggling Giants
and the soldiers of
the Castle Guard

The colourful
uniforms of the
Castle Guard shine
livelily during
ceremonial parade

The Second Courtyard originated only in the 16th century on the site of the former filled-in ditch. Today it is surrounded by uniform façades dating from the time of the Theresian reconstruction of the Castle which, however, conceal a complex architectural history. The Baroque fountain in the centre of the courtyard by the stonemason F. de Torre and the sculptor H. Kohl dates from 1686. Interesting was the development of the so-called Middle Wing between the 2nd and the 3rd Courtyards. In the first half ot the 12th century a Romanesque castle wall was erected on the site of the rampart of earlier date. The defence of the wall was enhanced by two towers, the more robust White Tower on the inside and the smaller Bishop's Tower on the outside. Emperor Rudolph II had a narrow corridor wing erected along the Romanesque wall in which part of his collections of works of art and curios were stored (Kunstkammer). The Middle Wing proper in its present width originated only in the second half of the 17th century.

The present-day appearance of the Chapel of the Holy Rood, jutting into the courtyard with the rounded East end, dates from the 19th century. In this chapel a part of the St. Vitus' treasure was exhibited in 1961—1990, a unique collection of liturgical objects, relics and memorial items dating from the 10th to the 19th centuries. The kernel of the treasure consists of the objects made in the reign of Emperor Charles IV (the coronation cross, the crystal can, the onyx goblet and others).

The former Renaissance stables on the ground floor of the Northern Wing were adapted to the Picture Gallery of Prague Castle. The original collection of paintings of Rudolph II is scattered all over Europe, and even the collection, renewed by Archduke Leopold Wilhelm in the second half of the 17th century, has not been preserved. The state was contributed to by frequent transfers of paintings between Prague and Vienna. In spite of these losses however, the Picture Gallery of Prague Castle contains the works of oustanding masters (H. von Aachen, B. Spranger, D. Tintoretto, Tizian, P. Cagliari called Veronese, P. P. Rubens, and others).

Below the West Wing archaelogical research discovered in 1950 the foundations of the church of Virgin Mary dating from the end of the 9th century.

From the Second Courtyard a passage with N. Pacassi's portal of 1772 leads to Powder Bridge in the north.

From the St. Vitus' treasure:
The so-called St. Wenceslas' helmet with an artistically decorated nose guard

The so-called St. Adalbert's mitre with pearl embroidery (13th century)

The Záviš' cross is richly decorated with enamel and filigree (mid-13th century)

Reliquary of the arm of St. George of gilded silver

The Baroque fountain
in the centre of the
courtyard is the work
of Francesco de Torre
and Hieronymus Kohl,
dating 1686

Overall view of the
Second Courtyard of
Prague Castle

The so-called
Middle Wing of
Castle buildings
and the east end of
the former court
Chapel of
Holy Rood

Installation of se-
lected objects from
the St. Vitus' trea-
sure in the interior
of the Chapel of
Holy Rood

Onyx goblet — a gift
of Charles IV to the
church, dating from
1350

The reliquary of
St. Sigismund is covered
with ivory reliefs

Gold cross, donated
to Charles IV by Pope
Urban V

The gold coronation cross is decorated with old cameos

Detail of decoration of one of the arms of the coronation cross

Jewel from the price-less chain from the period of Rudolph II (formerly a part of the so-called jewellery monstrance)

The reliquary bust of St. Vitus, made to the order of Vladislav Jagiello at the beginning of the 16th century
<<

Bust of another patron saint of the Kingdom of Bohemia, St. Adalbert
<

Veraikon, a Gothic plate painting with original painted frame

View of the Second Courtyard from Pacassi's gate in the Northern Castle Wing

View of the interior of the Picture Gallery of Prague Castle in the former stables of Rudolph II

This girl's portrait is the work of Hans von Aachen, one of the Rudolph's painters

Bust of Emperor Rudolph II in the Picture Gallery recalls the former treasures of his art collections

One of the exhibited portraits by Jan Kupecký (Portrait of Mrs. Schreyvogel)

Portrait of Jacob Kinig, German jeweller, by Paolo Cagliari, called Veronese

IACOBVS · KINIG · GERMANVS · FIESSENSIS ·

Venetian painting of
the 16th century is
represented also by
The Whipping of
Christ (Jacopo
Robusti, called
Tintoretto)

Tizian's Toilet of
a Young Lady is
probably the most
important item of
the collection

Bartholomaeus
Spranger, Allegory of
the Triumph of
Fidelity over Fate

St. Paul by
Petr Brandl represents the
paintings of Bohemian
High Baroque in the
Picture Gallery

The small picture,
The Parable of Tare
Sower, was painted by
Domenico Fetti

Detail of the largest
canvas of the Gallery,
the Gathering of
Olympians, by Peter
Paul Rubens

The site of the present St. Vitus' Cathedral was initially occupied by a four-apse rotunda of the same consecration, founded in the first third of the 10th century by Prince Wenceslas, later St. Wenceslas, chief patron saint of Bohemia. He himself was buried in the south apse of the rotunda and his grave was respected in all reconstructions and preserved in its initial place. After the middle of the 11th century Prince Spytihněv II decided to replace the rotunda with a three-aisled basilica with two galleries and two towers. The construction was completed in 1096. The basilica then served as the principal church of the Castle and of the whole kingdom until 1344, when the foundation stone of the Gothic cathedral was laid in the presence of King John of Luxembourg, his sons Charles and John Henry, Archbishop Arnošt of Pardubice and members of the clergy, the nobility and the knighthood. The first builder, Matthias of Arras, managed to build the ring of chapels and the pillars of the gallery before he died (1352). His successor, P. Parler of Gmund, erected the vault of the high chancel, the flying buttress system, the Golden Gate, the foundations of the big tower and of St. Wenceslas'Chapel, the central and most sacred part of the whole cathedral. It is decorated with polished precious stones and wall paintings dating from Charles' time and the beginning of the 16th century. The members of the royal family as well as the persons who have deserved for the construction of the church (archbishops, architects and construction directors) are portrayed by busts in the triforium which had become an original Gothic sculptural portrait gallery. The royal oratory dates from the Late Gothic period, while the B. Wohlmut's choir, initially closing the mediaeval part, and the copper roof of the principal tower represent Renaissance additions. The most important contribution of the Baroque is the silver tomb of St. John of Nepomuk (1733—1736). In 1859 the Association for the Completion of the Church was founded. The construction group, headed successively by J. Kranner, J. Mocker and K. Hilbert, completed the cathedral in 1929 in its present-day appearance. The interior was provided with a number of works of art (altars, wall paintings, reliefs, stained glass windows). In the triforium of the new part the gallery of church builders continues.

In 1990 the Cathedral was visited by Pope John Paul II (the first papal visit to the country).

The western façade of the St. Vitus' Cathedral is the most recent part of the whole building (completed in 1929)

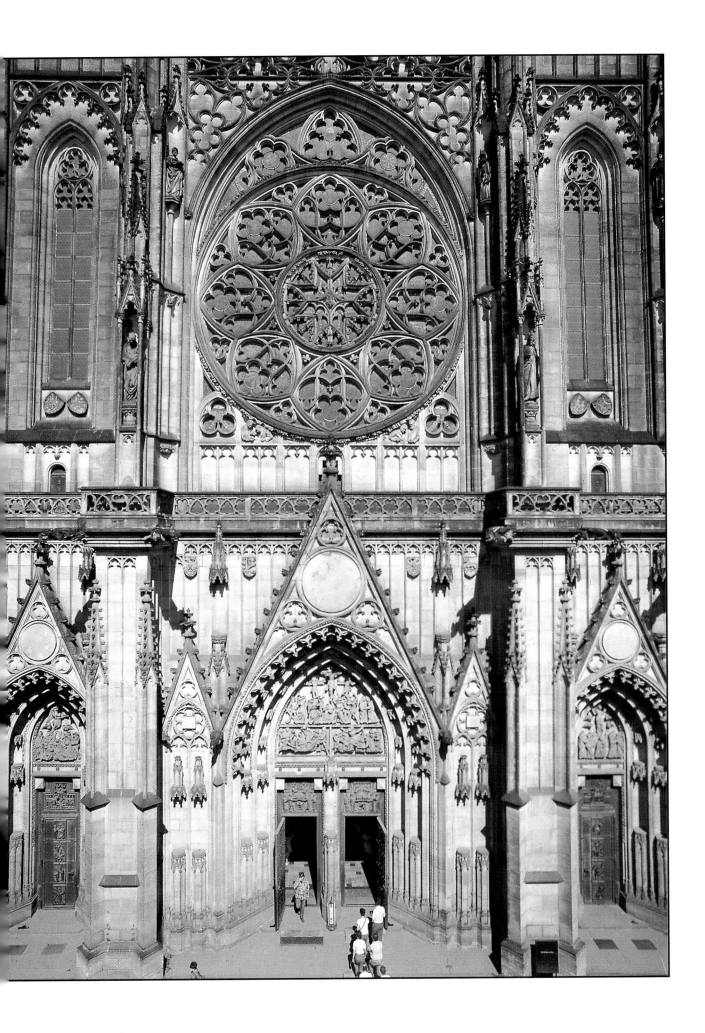

The Royal
Mausoleum with
the marble figures
of Ferdinand I,
Anne Jagiello and
Maximilian II

The rose window in
the west wall was
designed by
František Kysela.
Its subject is the
Creation of the
World
<<

The silver tomb of
St. John of Nepo-
muk dates from
1733 to 1736

<
The western tribune
affords the view of
the whole church
interior

The chancel with
the main altar and
the marble
Royal Mausoleum

The St. Wenceslas' Chapel is the most beautiful space of the Cathedral

During his visit to Prague Pope John Paul II met the representatives of the Church in the Cathedral

The Archbishop of Prague, Cardinal F. Tomášek, consecrating the chapel of St. Agnes of Bohemia in the western part of the Cathedral

The walls of the St. Wenceslas' Chapel are faced with polished precious stones and decorated with Gothic wall paintings

The statue of St. Wenceslas from 1373 is attributed to Peter Parler

The portrait bust of Charles IV, Roman Emperor and Bohemian King, in the internal triforium

The bust of Charles' IV third wife, Anne of Schweidnitz

Also the second builder of the Cathedral, Peter Parler, has his portrait in the internal triforium

The Bohemian
coronation jewels
are deposited in the
Crown Chamber of
the Cathedral,
closed by seven
locks

>
Drawing of Peter
Parler's vault in the
St. Wenceslas'
Chapel

>>
The wall paintings
on the northern wall
of the St. Wenceslas'
Chapel date
from the beginning
of the 16th century

The Old Sacristy has
the original rib vault
with two pendant
bosses
<<

The Wohlmut's choir
from 1557—1561 in-
itially closed the west-
ern end of the church
<

The individual chapels
of the St. Vitus'
Cathedral are lit by
remarkable stained
glass windows

This window was de-
signed by Alfons
Mucha. The subject is
the legend of the Sla-
vonic missionaries,
St. Cyril and
St. Methodius

The stained glass win-
dow in the transept
was designed by
Max Švabinský
on the subject of
The Last Judgement

The stone gargoyles in the old part of the Cathedral have the most bizarre shapes

The whole external buttress system is richly decorated with pinnacles, tracery and reliefs

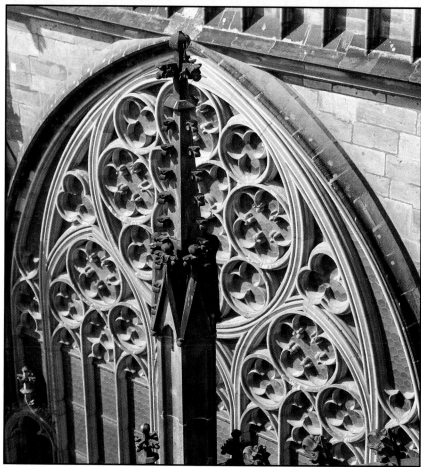

Also the new part of the Cathedral is decorated with numerous stone details

The weather cock, mounted on the transept roof (the cock is the attribute of St. Vitus to whom the Cathedral is consecrated)

The big St. Vitus' tower, Gothic in its kernel, was completed with the characteristic copper helmet in the Renaissance

The Third Courtyard was adapted to its present-day form by architect J. Plečnik in 1928—1931. Until that time the ground was of two different levels. Plečnik designed also the monolith of Mrákotín granite (memorial to the victims of the First World War, 1928), the new shape of the pedestal of the mediaeval sculpture of St. George and the Dragon, and the roofing of the excavations near the old Provost House. This house was the initial seat of the Bishops of Prague. Its East façade still displays the Romanesque window and stone masonry. From the Third Courtyard there was a ceremonial entrance to the St. Vitus' Cathedral (the so-called Golden Gate, decorated with the mosaic of the Last Judgement). On the opposite, i.e. on the South side of the courtyard, there is a portico with a balcony in the centre of a somewhat sobre classicist façade. The West façade of the Royal Palace was adapted in the same style under Maria Theresa. Its oldest part had served as the residence of the Princes of Bohemia as early as the 12th century. The palace gradually expanded and was radically reconstructed under Charles IV and Wenceslas IV. In 1493—1502 King Vladislav Jagiello commissioned its further reconstruction to B. Ried, who created one of the biggest and most beautiful secular Late Gothic spaces, the Vladislav Hall. Also the Equestrian Staircase and Luis (Ludvik's) Wing are Ried's works. From the windows of the latter the Governors (Jaroslav Bořita of Martinice and Vilém Slavata of Chlum) were thrown out in 1618 (Prague Defenestration which actually was the beginning of the Thirty Years War resulting in a terrible devastation of the whole Europe). The palace is connected with the All Saints' Chapel, the Gothic form of which disappeared in the fire of 1541. The present appearance is the result of the Renaissance reconstruction (1580). The impressive vault of the Old Diet is a more recent reminiscence of the Ried's vault (B. Wohlmut, 1559—1563). The walls and the vaults of the rooms of the New Land Rolls are decorated with the painted emblems of the highest officials of the realm and the Land Rolls officials. The past of Prague Castle, particularly its shape in the oldest periods, are discovered by archeological research. The finds include both the objects of every day use and rare jewels of gold and precious stones. Surprizingly rich were the finds in a 9th century burial ground beyond the Riding School building and the finds in the graves of the rulers.

The St. Vitus' Cathedral, the Old Provost House and the granite Monolith from 1928 in the Third Courtyard

<
The bronze statue of
St. George and the
Dragon is the work of
George and Martin of
Kluj, who cast it in
1373

Sculptural decorations
of the balcony
balustrade above
the entrance to the
South Wing
of the Castle

The façades of the wings
surrounding the Third Courtyard
have a uniform appearance,
imprinted on them by
the reconstruction in the reign
of Empress Maria Theresa

The eastern wall of the Vladislav Hall in the Royal Palace with the Renaissance portal leading to the choir of the All Saints' Chapel

The impressive interior of the Vladislav Hall, the work of B. Ried dating from 1490—1502

Since 1934
the elections of the
Presidents of the
Republic have been
taking place in the
Vladislav Hall

>
The Old Diet in the
Royal Palace was
the venue of the
sessions of the Diet
and of the
Land Court

The walls and the
vaults of the New
Land Rolls are
decorated with the
painted emblems of
the highest officials
of the Kingdom of
Bohemia
>

Ceremonial parade
on the Third
Courtyard after
Presidential election
on July 5, 1991

The emblem of the Kingdom of Bohemia from the rich vault of the socalled Vladislav's Bedchamber in the Royal Palace

The knights riding to the tournaments which took place in the Vladislav Hall ascended the Equestrian Staircase on horseback

<
The All Saints' Chapel obtained its present-day appearance by the reconstruction in 1580

The interior of the offices
of the Imperial Court Council
on the fourth floor
of the Luis Wing in the Royal Palace

Gold jewels from the archaeological research
of the burial ground
beyond the Riding School of Prague Castle,
dating from the 9th and 10th centuries

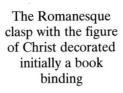
The Romanesque
clasp with the figure
of Christ decorated
initially a book
binding

A majolica stove tile
which formed part
of a sumptuous
Renaissance stove

Pottery dating from
the 16th century is
frequent among
archaeological finds

Gilded silver cross
decorated with
malachites which
was found in the
grave of
Maximilian II
(front and rear)

Ivory chess figure
dating from the
16th century

Anna Jagiello was
buried with a cap of
gold tinsel
<

Rings of
Anna Jagiello,
wife of Ferdinand I

Ring of Emperor
Rudolph II

The Order of the
Golden Fleece from
the grave of
Maximilian II

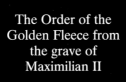

The eastern part of the Castle comprises various buildings in the most varied styles. The St. George's Basilica, the third oldest church in Prague Castle (founded before 921), was radically extended and rebuilt after the fire in 1142. The chancel with the principal apse, the crypt and both towers date from that time. Later on the Chapel of St. Ludmila with the Gothic tombstone of the saint, the south portal (about 1520) and the Chapel of St. John of Nepomuk (1718—1722) were added. The West façade facing the square is of Early Baroque origin, its colour scheme diverging from the standard of that time. The façade is decorated with a relief of St. George and with statues of Prince Vratislav and Princess Mlada.

Above the portal of the Chapel of St. John of Nepomuk there is a statue of two angels by F. M. Brokof.

The adjacent Convent founded in 973 (the oldest convent in Bohemia) was intended for the female branch of the Benedictine order. Its present appearance dates from the second half of the 17th century and from 1969—1975, when it was adapted to a gallery exhibiting the collections of Bohemian art of the Gothic, Renaissance and Baroque periods. The opposite front of St. George's Street consists in the vast building of the former Institute of Gentlewomen, founded by Empress Maria Theresa. It originated in 1753—1755 by the reconstruction of the Renaissance palace and garden of the Rožmberk family. The adjacent Lobkovicz Palace is an austere Early Baroque building dating from 1651—1668, erected on the site of the Renaissance residence of the Pernštejn family. The palace extends as far as the gate near the Black Tower — the only fully preserved tower of the Romanesque Castle fortifications (from the first half of the 12th century). The former Burgrave's House was the seat of the Chief Burgrave, who deputized for the Bohemian ruler during his absence from the country.

The north fortification above the Stag Moat was strenghened by Vladislav Jagiello by an outer wall with the Powder, White and Daliborka towers. To the north from the Burgrave's House there is the well-known Golden Lane.

Its picturesque tiny houses are the last remnants of the buildings which existed also in other parts of the Castle. The present-day Golden Lane was initiated by Rudolph II who permitted 24 Castle guards to build-up the blind arcades of the castle wall.

View of the eastern part of Prague Castle from the gallery of the St. Vitus' Cathedral

>
View of the interior of the Chapel of St. Ludmila, whose remnants were brought to the St. George's Basilica as early as 925

>>
Interior of the St. George's Basilica which has retained its original Romanesque character until the present day

The Romanesque relief with enthroned Madonna and donators is exhibited at present in the St. George's Basilica

View of the crypt below the chancel of the basilica

The Gothic tomb
of Prince Vratislav I,
the founder
of the church
(d. 921)

The recumbent
figure of Princess
Ludmila from the
Gothic tomb of this
saint

The Early Baroque
cloister of
St. George's
Convent

View from the cloister garth of the St. George's Convent, newly adapted during the reconstruction of 1969—1975, of the basilica towers

Exhibition of ancient Czech art in the interiors of the St. George's Convent
<

The picturesque houses in the Golden Lane were originally the abodes of the Castle gunners

>
In front of the eastern gate to Prague Castle and the Black Tower there is a favourite spot offering a magnificent view of Prague

In the north and in the south Prague Castle is surrounded with zones of gardens. The Royal Garden and practicaly the whole northern forefield were laid out by Ferdinand I. and connected with the Castle by a bridge spanning the Stag Moat. Its stone piers are still concealed in the bulky embankment. Near the northern bridge approaches there is the Early Baroque Riding School, built to the design of J. B. Mathey (1694—1695), with the main entrance gate to the Royal Garden opposite. The Royal Garden was partly reserved for decorative plants, partly for the cultivation, reproduction and acclimatization of exotic plants. Gradually it was provided with the buildings intended for the rest and entertainment of the court. Their number included, in the first place, the Summer Palace, the construction of which was begun by P. della Stella in 1538 and completed by B. Wohlmut in 1564. Also the Ballgame Hall, richly decorated with sgraffitoes, is the latter's work. The Baroque decorative features of the garden include the Hercules' Fountain, the Night sculpture in front of the Ballgame Hall, and the balustrade with lions and putti.

The garden around the Singing Fountain was reconstructed in the style of the Renaissance giardinetto by P. Janák in 1937—1939.

The southern garden originated on the site of the fortification of the outer bailey. The initial steep slope was levelled by bulky embankments. The oldest part is the so-called Paradise Garden, laid out as early as in the 16th century. From its older supplements only the Matthias' Pavilion (1617) has been preserved. On the copper roof of the round structure of the pavilion there is Matthias's monogram. The major part of the garden is the so-called Garden on the Ramparts bordering the whole southern front of the Castle. It dates from the second half of the 19th century. Its present form was designed by J. Plečnik in the twenties of our century. In the same period also the Paradise Garden was modified and provided with a monumental staircase and a decorative bowl made of a single piece of granite. In the Garden on the Ramparts J. Plečnik designed an observation terrace, an observation pavilion, the Bellevue colonnade and the modification of the Moravian Bastion.

Also the small Garden on the Bastion in front of the portico of the western entrance to the Spanish Hall is the work of J. Plečnik.

The statue of the Night in front of the Ballgame Hall in the Royal Garden is the work of the well known Baroque sculptor, M. B. Braun; its opposite number, the Day, was destroyed during the Prussian siege (1757)

>
The Garden on the Bastion was modified in 1930 by the design of Josip Plečnik

>>
The southern façade of the Royal Palace seen from the Garden on the Ramparts

The Riding School
terrace offers one of
the interesting views
of the Castle
<

One of the remain-
ders of the Baroque
decorations of the
Royal Garden is the
Hercules Fountain,
created by
J. J. Bendl (1670)

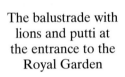

The Riding School
of Prague Castle,
built at the end of
the 17th century, is
used as exhibition
hall at present
<

The balustrade with
lions and putti at
the entrance to the
Royal Garden

The construction of
the Summer Palace,
which is an example
of pure Italian
Renaissance,
was started
by Paolo della Stella
in 1538 and
completed by
Bonifác Wohlmut
26 years later

The Singing
Fountain in front
of the Summer
Palace was cast by
Tomáš Jaroš,
the Court
Master Founder
(1564—1568)

The Paradise Garden at the southern foot of the Castle is laid out in the proximity of the observation ramp near the Hradčany Square

The Ballgame Hall in the Royal Garden, built by Bonifác Wohlmut in 1567—1569, has a façade richly decorated with sgraffitoes

View of the
St. Vitus' Cathedral
and a part of the
norhtern fortifica-
tion of the Castle
across the
Stag Moat

The windows of the Southern Wing
of the Castle afford a view of
the whole historical part of Prague

PRAGUE
CASTLE

Photos by Jiří Kopřiva
Text and arrangement by Petr Chotěbor
English translation by Slavoš Kadečka
Cover and graphic design by Karel Kárász
Published by Olympia Publishing House,
Prague, 1991, as its 2619th publication
1st English edition, 95 pages,
130 photos in colour
Responsible editor: Soňa Scheinpflugová
Technical editor: Zbyněk Zajíček
Printed by Polygrafia, Prague
27-074-91